THIS IS ME!

ME!

A WORLD INSIDE

Edited By Roseanna Caswell

First published in Great Britain in 2022 by:

Young Writers Est. 1991

Young Writers
Remus House
Coltsfoot Drive
Peterborough
PE2 9BF
Telephone: 01733 890066
Website: www.youngwriters.co.uk

Printed and bound in the UK by BookPrintingUK
Website: www.bookprintinguk.com
YB0492M

FOREWORD

*For Young Writers' latest competition This Is Me,
we asked primary school pupils to look inside
themselves, to think about what makes them unique,
and then write a poem about it! They rose to the
challenge magnificently and the result is this fantastic
collection of poems in a variety of poetic styles.*

*Here at Young Writers our aim is to encourage creativity
in children and to inspire a love of the written word, so
it's great to get such an amazing response, with some
absolutely fantastic poems. It's important for children to
focus on and celebrate themselves and this competition
allowed them to write freely and honestly, celebrating
what makes them great, expressing their hopes and
fears, or simply writing about their favourite things.
This Is Me gave them the power of words. The result
is a collection of inspirational and moving poems that
also showcase their creativity and writing ability.*

*I'd like to congratulate all the young poets
in this anthology, I hope this inspires them
to continue with their creative writing.*

CONTENTS

Sophie Bundy (8)	74
Joshua Pickering (8)	75
Omosileola (Charles) Olaniyan (8)	76
Elizabeth Peacey (6)	77
Jacob Mortimore (9)	78
Taliyah Boyce (7)	79
Sienna Richmond (8)	80
Victoria Fitzgibbons (10)	81
Penelope Fong (7)	82
Alex Eggitt (10)	83
William Mortimore (7)	84
Harriett Widdowson (9)	85
William Harris (7)	86
Benjamin Nokes (10)	87
Oliver Crossley-Fordham (9)	88
Tara Bluff (10)	89
Frankie Osborne (5)	90
Giles Highfield (9)	91
Scarlett Ross (9)	92
Alexander Drury (8)	93
William Hinchliffe (9)	94
Jayden Lee (7)	95
Ajay Uppal (8)	96
Jorawar Badh (7)	97
Ethan Jones (7)	98
Annabelle Brown (7)	99
George Christian (6)	100
Arya Basra (8)	101
Charlie Stanley (9)	102
Mila Curtis (11)	103
Lydia Godley (5)	104
Joshua Price-Stephens (6)	105
Xander Richmond (5)	106
Caitlyn Gibson (8)	107
Tobias Hodgson (6)	108
Thomas Hinchliffe (6)	109
Cassie Hather (7)	110
Dora Mayil (9)	111
Romie Fletcher (7)	112
Edward Gregory (6)	113
Finley Christian (7)	114
Ella Pashley (8)	115
Eliza Ardron-Levack (8)	116
Jenson Jones (5)	117
Bronwyn Jones (9)	118
Omosede Izehor (9)	119
Annabelle Layden (9)	120
Arya Luniya (8)	121
Esraa Wragg (5)	122
Matilda Hoad (6)	123
Seth Markham	124
Emily Brannan (6)	125
Robin Peirce (6)	126
Sophia Clarkson (7)	127
Ebony Dent (10)	128
Amelia Drury (7)	129
Oliver Pickering (7)	130
Lucy Barker (9)	131
Sebastian Aylmer (9)	132
Vivaan Bhounsle (8)	133
Theo Millington (10)	134
Sarah Mirza (7)	135
Robyn Close (5)	136
Reuben Bennett (5)	137
Willow Powell (9)	138
Isabel Price-Stephens (6)	139
Moses Ilori (7)	140
Ayesha Thomas (6)	141
Henry Burkitt (7)	142
Nahla Walton (6)	143
Felix Cameron (8)	144
Adhya Chandra (6)	145
Henry Barlow (5)	146
Micah Luhanga (5)	147
Noah Otley (7)	148
Dexter Hewson (7)	149
Louis Jesson (7)	150
Sophia Dudgeon (7)	151
Emily Blunt (7)	152
Bella Damary-Wilson (7)	153
Ayda Davallo (6)	154

Lawrence Community Primary School, Wavertree

Amelia Miah (9)	155
Maisha Miah (9)	156

Mary Exton Primary School, Hitchin

Lexie Bechman (8)	158
Tilda Bechman (10)	159
Grace Degnan-Gordon (10)	160
Aaryahi Pathak (7)	162
Ivy Knowles (9)	163
Evelyn Wilcox (7)	164
Isla Skeggs (10)	165
Daisy Buckridge (8)	166
Isabella Boyle (8)	167
Bryony Hall (10)	168
Beatrix Hyde (7)	169
Lucie Rayner (9)	170
Lexie Marie Copp (9)	171
Charlie Carrick (7)	172
Olly Backhouse (7)	173
Emma Sanchez Andreu (9)	174
Annabel Davies (9)	175
Freya Knowles (7)	176
Rhia Mather-Howard (9)	177

Our Lady's Catholic Primary School, Dartford

Alicja Targos (10)	178
Nathaniel Salazar (11)	180
Oreoluwa Olawoye (10)	182
Nifemi Omisade (10)	183
Courtney Anyaegbuna (10)	184
Marcus Lawal (9)	186
Kaycee Cassandra Duenas (10)	187
Santy Ofosu-Asamoah (10)	188
Azoma Egeruka (9)	189

Ruislip Gardens Primary School, Ruislip

Audrey Serafin (8)	190
Bleu Cass (8)	192
Bella-Rose Rogers (8)	194
Erin Carter (8)	195
Freya Lucia Patel (8)	196
Mia Manning (8)	197
Antony Caron (8)	198
Danii Reguretsky (8)	199
Eduardo Martins Aguiar (8)	200
Ashlee Doorga (8)	201
Summer Gambell (8)	202
Fallon Hewitt (8)	203
Hugo Bwalya (8)	204
Ruby Freeman (9)	205
Peyia McCarville (8)	206
Matilda Cotton (9)	207
Joseph Leach (8)	208
Joud Hobi (8)	209
Aiden Smit (8)	210
Whaj Al Karam (8)	211
Tilly Rose Evans (8)	212
Maria Frankie (9)	213
Leiliana Rai (8)	214
Maya Marcoci (8)	215
Alfie Lynas (8)	216
Betsy Llewellyn (8)	217
Yamin Al Youssef (8)	218
George Rycraft (8)	219
Mekhi Perry (9)	220
Harold Liko (8)	221

The Japanese School In London, Acton

Kyo Adachi-Mavromichalis (11)	222
Hikari Inoue (11)	223
Yuika Kaji (10)	224
Tomoharu Shigetomi (11)	225
Yuto Murata (10)	226
Shin Inada (10)	227
Ray Nestor Ito (11)	228

THE POEMS

All About Me

My name is Sophie
My favourite colour is pink
I hate brown
I also love yellow
It reminds me of the sun
I love my family
I also love art
When I grow up, I want to be an actor
I really, really love Jump in Joy
I love my teacher
My favourite animals are polar bears
I like school
My favourite holiday is Christmas
My favourite subject is science
My favourite holiday is in Blackpool
And this is me!

Sophie Ritchie (8)
Craigbank Primary School, Sauchie

Recipe!

To make me, you will need:
My best friend, Reagan
Some loombands
Gymnastics
A bit of Lego
French bulldogs
Not too much spice
And not too much sweetener
All my friends, family and teachers and P4
A pinch of fun

Bake for twenty minutes
Mix all together
Add some strawberries for decoration
This is me!

Kayci Salmond (8)
Craigbank Primary School, Sauchie

Funny Sunny Me!

I am all about...
Butter and jam toast
Cute Pomeranian
Funny jokes
Rice and stew
Lots of yummy food
I'm as smart as Albert Einstein
I'm sometimes silly
I'm sometimes bold
I love fun activities
I love lots of friends
I'm always messy
I love sport
And I will always be me!

Idianosa Ajayi (8)
Craigbank Primary School, Sauchie

Alexander

A pples are my favourite fruit
L ife is good
E xcited to be a judo coach
X box is great fun
A nd so is tag
N ew wrestlers are really nice
D ogs are the best
E specially my dog, Max
R angers are my team.

Alexander Rae (8)
Craigbank Primary School, Sauchie

My Wobbly Tooth

W obbly

O w that hurts

B rush my teeth

B ig tooth coming in next

L iked tooth

Y ank out tooth

T ooth

O h no, my tooth is coming out

O ut tooth

T ooth is out

H ooray!

Jessica Grieve (8)
Craigbank Primary School, Sauchie

Let's Talk About Me

I swim through the sea
Like a beautiful narwhal
Blowing water out of its blowhole
My favourite colour is blue
Like the horizon blending into the sunset
Reading is like sinking into the ocean
And being yourself and having
Peace and quiet in your jammies.

Jorja Preston (8)
Craigbank Primary School, Sauchie

What About You?

My favourite colour is blue
What about you?
I like to swim really, really fast
I am smart
My favourite subject is maths
I am funny
I am messy
My hero is Michael Jackson
On DVD, my favourite thing
To see is Coraline.

Ailsa Strachan (8)
Craigbank Primary School, Sauchie

Recipe

To make me:
A handful of my friends
A teaspoon of loombands
A cup of my dog
Two handfuls of my family
A pinch of kindness
And a bucket full of love

I can love a lot of things
If you give me the right recipe.

Reagan Phillips (8)
Craigbank Primary School, Sauchie

This Is Khyla!

I like to earn my tags at taekwondo
Twice a week is when I go

I'm a wee bit bossy and a little bit shy
I like to look up in the sky

My baby cousin likes to play with boats
He is noisy as a goat.

Khyla Salmond (8)
Craigbank Primary School, Sauchie

I Will Never Change Who I Am!

I am funny sometimes
I like doughnuts too
How about you?
I love the colour red
I am happy all the time
I love my friends and family
My hero is my mummy
Because she is there for me.

Frayah McLaren (8)
Craigbank Primary School, Sauchie

Sunny Me!

C razy

A mbitious

M cDonald's fan

E xploding with excitement

R iding on my penny board

O n my couch every day watching the TV

N oticeable.

Cameron Manton (8)

Craigbank Primary School, Sauchie

I Like Football

I like playing football with my friends
I get hit in the head
I tripped over the ball
I hit the goalie in the face
I hit the crossbar
I scored in top bins!

Josh Thomson (8)
Craigbank Primary School, Sauchie

This Is Abi

I am smart

A m friendly
M assive brain

A lways will take the risk
B rave
I ntelligent and very kind.

Abi McMillan (8)
Craigbank Primary School, Sauchie

This Is My Life

I like Celtic
My hero is Obama
I have a boyfriend
I like art and poems
I love my family and friends
I like music and movies.

Mally Whyte (8)
Craigbank Primary School, Sauchie

This Is Emeli

E xciting, I am
M aking people happy
E xcellent at making friends
L ikes dogs
I ntelligent.

Emeli Thomson (8)
Craigbank Primary School, Sauchie

Me!

M essy

I ntelligent

L ikes dogs

L ikes making friends

I ncredible

E xcited.

Millie McFarlane (8)

Craigbank Primary School, Sauchie

All About Eleanor

My name is Eleanor, I bet you know
There's a lot to tell, best make a brew
First, there's my sister, she's quite a pain
My dad is the same
They're both annoying, without a doubt
But that's what some of your family is about
Then comes my mum, who loves a hug
She can be frustrating, without a doubt
But when she sings, she never shouts
I have six pets, so there's no need to pout
Two cats, two guinea pigs and two budgies
to count
I'd like a puppy because they're so cute
But my dad's a pain without a doubt
My favourite sports are hockey and swimming
I like to compete and, of course, love winning
I play the guitar, the piano and sing
Orchestra and choir give me the chance to swing
I think I'm courageous, loving and funny
I make a good friend because I'm always sunny.

Eleanor Idle-Crane (10)

Hill House School, Auckley

K-Pop Industry

The first K-pop I noticed was BTS in 2017
Their concept 'love yourself'
Is as motivational as learning a new language
Next was Red Velvet
In early 2020, I saw them in a movie
And decided to become a Reveluv
Next, it was Blackpink
Around the BTS Dynamite era
Saw four amazing vocalised girls
And decided to become a Blink
However, the fandom is as toxic as acid
Oops! I forgot about Mamamoo in early 2020
I heard one of the member's solos
And looked more into the group
Being as funny as a dancing goat
I decided to become a Moo Moo
In early 2021, was TXT and Enhypen
TXT was like the brother of BTS
And Enhypen as the cousin
Later was Twice, Itzy and Weekly
Saw some songs of theirs on TikTok

And explored more
Twice, as sweet as flowers
Itzy, like soldiers
Weekly, as happy as the sun
Lastly, IU, she isn't in a group
But is a solo artist
My favourite solo artist, in fact
Her face is as innocent as a child
And she loves to smile
She may have one of the best vocals in K-pop
I wonder who I will see next.

Divine Ilori (11)
Hill House School, Auckley

All About Me

Up in the mountains is where I like to be
The mountain range fills me with glee
My puppy's tail wagging and she too agrees
The mountains are where I love to be

A farmer's daughter, with curly blonde hair
Fashion does not bother me, I really don't care
Jumping in the corn is my best dare
It feels like I am falling in thin air

You may see me in the village
On my roller skates, at speed
It's even more fun when I'm holding my puppy's
lead
My friends have caught the roller skating bug,
I must say thanks to me
Thank you, Father Christmas, for putting them
under the tree

At home there are many things I love to do
Singing, sewing, baking and puppy training too
Cricket and hockey are sports to me that are new
I'll have a go at anything, and that statement is
true!

When I grow up, I want to be a vet
I can think of nothing better than caring for other people's pets
I know I will have to work hard, and always do my best
It's a good job I don't need to rest.

Sophie Dent (9)
Hill House School, Auckley

Recipe How To Bake A Lulu

Ingredients:
A large spoonful of dreams
One full cup of sparkling smiles
One extra large caring heart
Two helping hands
10ml of imagination
A handful of determination
A sprinkle of good vibes
A handful of history
A full pot of loyalty

To make this recipe
You must be in a crazy, comfy home
In an ancient Roman bowl
Empty a handful of history
10ml of imagination, determination and loyalty
Mix well with the helping hands
Gently stir in the good vibes
Making sure that no bad vibes try to sneak in
Add the full caring heart, making sure you don't break it

Now bake for ten years in a 140cm tin in a warm
heat
Once ready, decorate with locks of golden hair
Bright blue eyes, a dash of curiosity and a
sparkling smile
Sprinkle with happiness
Serve with a generous amount of warm hugs
And this makes me!

Lulu Goulden (9)
Hill House School, Auckley

How To Make Me!

You will need:
A room full of pink tutus
A gallon of sparkling water
A cricket bat full of determination
A handful of sass
A dash of fun
A lot of happiness
A slab of cucumber
Some tomatoes fresh from the vine
One happy smile
And a pinch of magic

Now you need to:
Add a gallon of sparkling water
Mix in a room full of pink tutus
Stir with the cricket bat full of determination
Add a handful of sass and a pinch of fun
Don't forget about the slab of cucumber
Mash with the cricket bat until smooth
Pour onto the tray and bake for two minutes
Take out and cool for one minute
Add tasty tomatoes fresh from the vine for garnish

And sprinkle with a lot of happiness
Then add one happy smile
Finally, add a pinch of magic!
Abracadabra, you have made me!

India Leach (9)
Hill House School, Auckley

Wilfred, My Dream Dog!

Wilfred is my dream dog
When I think about him
The perfect picture is in my mind
But this is not a poem
Where I describe him to you
I want to tell you about his life...
Every day, we wake up
I cuddle him close to me
I'll tell him fun stories about my dream
While I groom his soft, silky, greyish fur
Next, I will make him breakfast
His favourite treats, of course
Then I go to work
And start to miss him more and more
When I get home, I clip on his leash
And take him on his favourite walk
Around the best park
We get home at 4.50
And get ready to watch our favourite films
At 6.00, we eat our tea

And take some snacks for later
Then we go upstairs to play some games
And get our energy out before we go to bed.

Cerys Pritchard (10)
Hill House School, Auckley

Adventure Holidays

Summertime is full of rhyme
Off on holiday, towards the beach sign
The sun is ever glowing
It is never snowing

Eating ice cream on the promenade
Next to London to see the Shard
In Nelson's Square, the lions roar
And in the zoo, wolves paw

In Paris is the Eiffel Tower
My challenge is to climb it in an hour
Louvre gallery is full of amazing art
The glass pyramid architect is so smart

Disneyland in the USA
Is where Mickey, Donald and Pluto play
In Washington is the White House
It is too grand just for a mouse

On a plane to Italy, seeing ancient arches
Tourists at the Colosseum and walking through
ancient parks
Home to England, after a long holiday
Back home on the motorway!

Emma Cutts (10)
Hill House School, Auckley

This Is Me

Something I'm proud of that I must tell you,
Is that I am in the house of blue!
If you ask me good things about it I'll say
Positive things for more than a day.
I'm very athletic and love basketball,
If only I was a bit more tall.
I can imagine looking up at the stars,
Looking at planets far from ours.
You never know what's out there
If you just look up and stare.
Until the clouds cover the secrets away
Trust me, they'll be there to stay.
I want to know when we will be able to see the sun
And share my predictions with everyone.
I love to represent my team,
To make their faces light up and beam.
I play the cornet and it's cool
But, I love my house the most
So three cheers for school!

Lilian Carmo (8)

Hill House School, Auckley

Who Am I?

People see what they want to see
But do they even care about what I want to be?
Every day, the pressure is so high
It's like a giant rock on my back that's fallen from the sky
Meeting new people is the best part of my day
It's because I can tell them who I am
Without them judging me in a mean way
It's so irritating when people give you a label
I mean, it's like I have just been hit by a table
Sometimes, I feel like people are so much more than that
We are not just a one-trick pony with a labelled top hat
So, let me be who I am
Without you telling me or choosing for me
So I have to ask you non-stop who am I?
I am who I am and if you can't accept that
Then who are you and who am I?

Yuanzi Wang (11)
Hill House School, Auckley

We're All Special

My name is Isaac
I am nine years old
I am your typical kid
If truth be told

I do my homework
I go to school
And have swimming lessons
At the local pool

Outside of school
I love to play
And hope to be
A vet someday

I know I'll be an awesome vet
Because I'm crazy about my pet
But not just about my lovely dog
But all animals, big and small

My name is Isaac
And on second thought
I'm not your typical kid
I like to be bold

I do martial arts
I play the guitar
And maybe one day
I'll be a rockstar

I think we're all special
In our own way
Let's make each other happy
And everything will be okay.

Isaac Birdsall (9)
Hill House School, Auckley

Tori Leigh

T ors is my nickname to my close family and friends

O n holiday at a nice sunny place like Tenerife or Majorca is my favourite place to be

R eading Harry Potter and getting lost in another world is how I like to spend my nights

I love acting and have lots of fun singing and dancing in plays

L oving, kind, generous young lady I hope I am

E ager to learn new stuff in history and explore my favourite topics

I love making memories with my friends and our midnight feasts at sleepovers I will never forget

G oing to Meadowhall with my pocket money is my favourite thing to do when the weather is dull and black

H ill House is the school I attend with all my friends.

Tori Jones (9)
Hill House School, Auckley

The Show Has Begun

I walked onto the ice-cold stage
As I grabbed the mic
I felt a cold shiver run down my spine
The butterflies inside me fluttered around
My stomach like marbles in a tub
My mouth opened and I trembled
The words left my mouth
"Ladies and gentlemen..."
I felt a cold breeze as the curtains opened
The piano started
And my breath echoed around the room
That was now filled with beady little eyes
The ensemble started singing
Bright, beautiful blue lights glowed in the dark
The atmosphere was like nothing I had ever
felt before
Soon, I heard my cue
And with one final breath
I whispered, "The show has begun!"

Amber Oldham (10)
Hill House School, Auckley

My Cats

M y first cat is called Tabby
Y es, I have three cats, they make me happy

T he school I go to is the best
H ockey is the best
R eading I like a lot
E ating food when I am sad makes me happy again
E ating fruit gives me energy

C uddles from my cats are so amazing
U p in the tree in my garden, I like to read
T V is my favourite way to relax
E ven though I may look sad, I'm always happy inside

C ats rule my house
A fter school activities are the best
T alking with people makes me happy
S ummer is the best season ever.

Charlotte Morgan (10)

Hill House School, Auckley

Stunt Scooter

S liding swiftly on the smooth tarmac, I went to the quarter pipe

T rying to bunny-hop off the quarter pipe

U sing the ramp on the other side to do bar spin

N ot wobbling even a bit

T remendously, I finished the trick, landing on my rear wheel

S lowly I got my scooter for another jump

C arefully lined it up on the quarter pipe

O h, this could hurt if it went wrong

O ww! I fell off my scooter, shocked by the fall

T his time, I was going to pull off the trick

E ventually, I got to jump correctly

R esting time, I finished at the quarter pipe.

James Baxter (10)

Hill House School, Auckley

A Soul That Is Dark And Light

My soul is light but dark
It confuses me
Outside, I'm a burning flair
But inside I'm ashes
If I get called names or pushed
My demons come out
From the darkness inside me
And flourish, they control my feelings
And emotions for the rest of the day
I get back from school
My mum looked at me
And asked if I was okay
She gave me a hug
And the demons ran away
Back into the darkness
Hiding for a chance to return
My flair shines brightly again
Filled with happiness
So it doesn't matter

If you are happy or sad
It matters on what you choose to be
And that would be the real you.

Jude Dickinson (11)

Hill House School, Auckley

Just Me!

So here I go, trying to describe me and what
I like to do
Piano, gymnastics, ballet to name just a few
I love to dance and practice as much as I can
Miss Lucy is my teacher and I am her number
one fan
I am learning piano and I really love to play
But, being honest, my favourite is gymnastics,
jazz and ballet
I hope one day, I can be in a West End show
I am going to practice and practice until I am a pro
Performing under the lights would be a dream
come true
Jumping and dancing perfectly on cue
I want to do gymnastics near and afar
One day, my name will shine brightly and I'll
be a superstar!

Autumn McEwen (5)
Hill House School, Auckley

This Is Who I Am...

Z any and charming, making her friends laugh

A lways smiling and helpful sharing everything in half

H er nature is so kind and her personality is amazing

R aring to delve into all challenges

A lways giving 100% and trying her best

M otivating others and aiming high

A lways reaching the top and attempting to fly

H er smile brightens the room and her voice is so melodious

M any adore her cheeky grin

O ften wanting to be like her

O thers wish to be her friends as she cares more for them than herself

D aring kind and adventurous little girl.

Zahra Mahmood

Hill House School, Auckley

Football

Walking onto the field, heads held high
The crowd roaring, come on the boys

Hoofing the ball up the pitch
The first goal soon went in
The boys went to celebrate, come on, keep going

We scored once again
The opponents feeling the pain
Two became three, three became four

We need to stay calm, focus, focus, come on
Don't stop, keep calm, only five minutes to go

There we go, the whistle we all wanted to hear
Let's celebrate, let's celebrate like never before

What a game, well played to the opponents
But it's fair to say, we won fair and square.

Harry Ogley (11)
Hill House School, Auckley

This Is Me!

T o be honest, who cares what people think?

H ow can people just not let their personalities shine like the incandescent sun

I f you know you're not being yourself, don't be scared to show the real you

S till not being you? You are who you are and no one can change that

I am me and you are you, so just own your personality for once

S o what if people say you're different from them, that's good, be your own person

M any people are scared to show their personalities and that's not right

E veryone just be brave and bold, be you!

Felicity Ward (8)
Hill House School, Auckley

Bake A Jess Cake!

Preheat to 30°C, Jess cakes don't like the cold
To start off, you'll need a pinch of humour
Now add a cup of independence
Next, add a teaspoon of flexibility
Then add a cup of love for horse riding
For your sixth ingredient
Pour three cups of friendship into the mixture
Now add four cups of family
Next, add a sprinkle of impatience
Crack five fun eggs into the batter
Then add a pinch of creativity
Add six cups of clumsiness
For number twelve
Add two cups of love for movies
Now mix
Put in the oven for fifteen minutes
And then enjoy your Jess cake!

Jess Burnett (10)
Hill House School, Auckley

This Is Me

I am annoying because
I sometimes ask too many times
For the thing I really want
And I already got given the answer no
I am hard-working because
I can finish all of my maths
In under twenty minutes
And I love homework
I am sometimes funny
And joke around often
I am kind and polite to my peers
But can sometimes
Do the wrong thing without even knowing
I am fit and healthy
I haven't drunk an unhealthy drink for four weeks
I am like gold shining in a risky yellow tomb
I earn treats and rewards
As well as a really nice birthday.

Daniel Crampton (8)
Hill House School, Auckley

My Cat, Rosie

M ad half hours every day

"Y ikes!" She caught a mouse... again

C razy and cunning in every way

A lways ready for food

T ries her best to fit into small, uncomfortable-looking spaces... eg. my lunchbox

R olling around in the grass, catching mice is one of her favourite things to do

O verall, she's just lonely

S leeping on my bed is her favourite

I love my cat, however, she's too crazy for this world

E very single pet in the world, combined, would never make up to Rosie.

Elizabeth Barlow (10)
Hill House School, Auckley

This Is Me

With my little hands and little toes
My brown hair and button nose
My family have seen me grow
Into the boy, they now know

I love my football, watching and playing
My real love is flying
Whether on a jet to a faraway place
Or paragliding high above the sea
To make my heart race

I love life beneath the waves in scuba gear
That is something I could do all year
I love adventure, of any kind
Or anything to expand my mind

I love my family
They are always there
To support me
And take me everywhere.

Ayaan Mahmood (10)
Hill House School, Auckley

All About Me!

I love to bake, it's super fun
All day long, especially with my mum
Yummy, yummy cakes are so cool
If I mess up, I am not a fool
I love watching Disney movies
While my dad makes me some super smoothies
Tennis is the sport I like to play
And my mum and dad play with me all day
My dog is super cute and fluffy
But she is a little bit chubby
I am very independent, look at me go
I am on a very love level in gymnastics though
Just like Rapunzel, I am a blondie
But when I wake up in the morning
I am like a zombie.

Hollie Booth (9)
Hill House School, Auckley

Me, Myself And Me

How best to describe me and what I love to do?
I enjoy travel, music, my iPhone and football too
London and Dubai are my most favourite
places to go
Football is my treasured game and one day
I will turn pro
I follow Celtic through the good times and the bad
Although Celtic have been losing recently, it is
rather sad
Then there is my iPhone that I love with all
my heart
Lots of games, apps, messages... We are
never apart
All in all, I am happy as can be
I have great friends and family who love me
for being me.

Caden McEwen (9)
Hill House School, Auckley

Legoland

L ego leaping across the alive room of creations and wonders

E ndangered animal, the poor red panda fighting wildfires

G reen from hard work and what it does

O rigami, from animals to boats to even planes, paper of old creations of the past

L and of the leaping leopard landing on the spot on the gravel in the Africa planes

A nimals awakening from the spot of the light in the jungle

N etball and sport is my speciality

D ogs, two, in fact, named Mulberry and Henry, I love them more than everything.

Finlo Irvine (8)

Hill House School, Auckley

The Recipe To Create Nathish

Ingredients:
Two gallons of my family
One and a half gallons of my friends
One teaspoon of pizza
One and a half teaspoons of Lego
Half a tablespoon of rugby
One and a half tablespoons of Minecraft
Two tablespoons of YouTube
One tablespoon of dinosaurs
One and a half tablespoons of Netflix

Recipe:
First, lightly stir my family and friends
Then sprinkle rugby on
Dump pizza and Lego
And roughly stir
Then, pour in YouTube and Netflix
And smear dinosaurs and Minecraft all over it.

Nathish Thivakaran (10)
Hill House School, Auckley

My Olympic Dream!

S woosh, I plunge into the glistening blue pool

W iggling my legs underwater, I glide at speed back up to the surface

I mmediately, my arms and legs working together, pulling me powerfully through the water

M ovement to my right, my fellow swimmers are hot on my heels

M ovement to my left, the crowd roaring us on

I t's neck and neck, it'll be down to the final length

N early there, an extra push for the last few metres

G old medal! Yes, my Olympic dream has come true.

Benjamin Ogley (9)

Hill House School, Auckley

Recipe Poem!

To create me, you will need:
A yellow bedroom as bright as the sun
Five rabbits as small as ants
One gloomy, dark, black cat as glorious as gold
A load of ham and pineapple pizza
An annoying brother, a kind and helpful mother
and a funny father
A gleaming, tidy bedroom as shiny as Mr Clean's
head

Next, you will need:
A tiny bit of sadness
100g of fun and weird
20g of mischievousness
Mix with gold and blue-grey icing
Add lots of sprinkles of happiness
Stir and the magic is done.

Isabella Wade (8)
Hill House School, Auckley

Tiberius

T his is me. I like to play football with all my friends

I am hard-working and I try my best at school

B eing me, no one else can be me because everyone's different

E lephants are one of my favourite animals

R overs, I support a football team called Doncaster Rovers

I love having McDonald's as their food tastes awesome

U niversal Studios is one of my dream places I want to go to in the future

S porty, I love and do lots of sports and my favourite is football.

Tiberius Batchelor (8)

Hill House School, Auckley

Cricket

I love cricket, it is my favourite sport
Kitted out in all white with helmet and pads
for support
Filled with excitement and joy at every match
Will I hit a six, bowl the stump or even get a catch?
When I was captain, it made me delightful
Winning matches and trophies is always prideful
Doncaster Town Cricket is where it all began
My desire is to play like Ben Stokes
I'm his biggest fan
Everyone in my family loves cricket
Why wouldn't they?
Cricket is the best sport.

Elycee Patel (10)
Hill House School, Auckley

Laria

H   appiness and joy is what I like most

A   lways willing to help where help is needed

P   leasantness costs nothing

P   erformance and competition are great... but I don't like losing

I   ndeed, me and you have so much more than others, why not share

N   ot for my looks, but for what I do is what I would like to be known

E   verybody needs some help sometimes

S   weet, dreamy and playful... I believe in fairies

S   port is games and games are fun.

Laria Halbeisen (9)

Hill House School, Auckley

This Is Me!

T he thing that is most important to me is my family

H elping out is good but you should do the thing that you do best

I am the best daughter in the world

S ass is a part of the puzzle that makes me

I can ignite myself and stand in front of the crowd

S mall as a mouse but as clever as a mathematician

M agnifying glasses make things bigger, but I make it brighter

E xcellent bike rider, I stopped with stabilisers when I was three!

Ruhi Naiya Odedra (8)

Hill House School, Auckley

This Is Why I Make Me, Me

E veryone is my friend

L ittle but very loud

A dventurous, brave and likes to explore loads of creepy places

I ntelligent but sometimes messes up and gets things wrong

N ight owl that likes to sleep in the morning

A nimal lover who adores cats

M onkey that loves to climb trees

I ndependent and free to do things how I like

A rtistic and likes to draw and paint pictures

H ectic and full of fun and exciting surprises.

Ellie Miah (9)

Hill House School, Auckley

All Bout Me

My name is Isla, I'm nine years old
I love to dance, I'm so bold
I see myself as caring
I see myself so daring
I'm just someone who is outgoing
I enjoy gymnastics which I find fantastic
With the jumps and the kicks
And the forward rolls in the mix
I enjoy going to school where you can't be a fool
You are encouraged by the teachers to do well
And they come across as cool
This is my poem, this is all about me
I will agree that this is a recipe of me.

Isla-Brooke Raradza (9)
Hill House School, Auckley

I Am Ivana

I have a family like no other because they always support me

A t any time, I'll always love Nutella because it helps my sweet tooth

M y favourite event is Halloween because I get sweets

I will always be an artist because it is my dream to be an artist

V icious sometimes but also sweet because I'll always have a good heart

A lways a Tom Fletcher book fan

N ever going to not like purple

A utumn, adventurous artist.

Ivana Iwu (7)

Hill House School, Auckley

Friendship Makes Me!

T ogether, we have fun
H aving the best time of our lives
I nterests we share and things we get done
S inging our favourite songs with lots of high-fives

M ixing our best-loved coloured paint
A nd making it into art
K ind, just like a saint
E very day is a fresh start
S lime, we enjoy making it

M y friends and I play whenever we get time
E veryone is done, along with this rhyme.

Erin Xhemali (9)
Hill House School, Auckley

Neeko, My Cat

Neeko, my cat, likes to hide
He's probably thinking about tonight
He's an excellent teleporter
As well as a food moaner

As fluffy as a fluffball
Cuddles, we like to call
Stretches then sits under a tree
But where does he do the loo?

Neeko loves his poses
A doughnut, a loaf, and even a noodle
Neeko goes miaow to the fridge
Because he knows where the milk goes

We go on walks, he follows too
Neeko, we all love you!

Rayna Rajasundaram (8)
Hill House School, Auckley

Football

They jumped upon an ambulance
During cheers and drunken chants
With no respect, no sense of pride
"Football's coming home!" they cried

Others had too much booze
Got carried away and left with a bruise
Upon a fragile cheek, they kissed
A drunken blow, a drunken fist

"Three lions on a shirt!" they cried
But acted with no sense of pride
It's unacceptable to act so grim
Whether England lose or win.

Charlie Lockwood (11)
Hill House School, Auckley

Our Family

I love my family, we have so much fun together

S o many laughs with smiles that last forever

A fter school with my brother, we will make a den inside

B ut when my mum says it is bath time, we sometimes try to hide

E very night, we read our favourite books

L ike the one about the boy called Stanley, who cooks

L ife at our house is so very sweet

E specially if Dad's in charge of choosing bedtime treats.

Isabelle Hanley (6)

Hill House School, Auckley

My Favourite Superhero

My favourite superhero
Is cool, clever and quick
You might think he's just an animal
I think he's kinda slick
He was faster than a moose
And as powerful as Zeus
He's a really quick fighter
But he's still getting lighter
He's an athletic fiend
He has many friends
But not Mr Bean
My favourite superhero
He's got a really hi-tech house
My favourite superhero
Is the one and only
Danger Mouse!

Jacob Burrows (8)
Hill House School, Auckley

This Is Me

I am curious because
I have a big imagination
And this is me
I am friendly because
I am loyal to my friends
And I love mice
I am fun and entertaining
Happy and joyful because
I love doing things freely and wildly
I am special, calm and nice
I'm playful and sweet because
I like to play with my friends
I am helpful, I try
And I'm hardworking
I'm a bit shy
And cannot talk in front of lots of people.

Elizabeth Alexander (8)
Hill House School, Auckley

This Is Me!

T otally hard-working, I am ready to go
H elpful and kind, I am as beautiful as an eagle
I am a chocoholic and I love to read
S ometimes I get a little mischievous though

I love baking but I always taste the mixture
S ensible and competitive, I am as cuddly as a teddy bear

M um and I always play tennis in my grandparent's garden
E njoying the weather, I am as bright as the sun!

Aneesa Hussain (8)

Hill House School, Auckley

Me, Myself And I

My name is Luke
A happier boy you could never meet
Numbers and letters are not my game
Friendly, kind and loving
With a passion for family, friends, music
And don't forget the mighty Blades
I like to drum to the beat of the music
Singing at the top of my voice
To Grandad's Frank Sinatra
Dad's Jam, Mum's Prince
And my Ed Sheeran
On the radio, I dream to be
Playing all my tunes
What will yours be...?

Luke Bowman (10)
Hill House School, Auckley

All About Me

I sing 'Lavender's Blue' beautifully

Z oo is where I visit happily

M ay is the month of my birthday

A boriginal people are what I learnt about yesterday

J uice is my favourite drink

A las! My mummy doesn't agree with me, I think

W aiting for me every day is my baby brother

A dorable, cute and a little drooly

D oesn't matter, we both love each other!

Izma Jawad (6)

Hill House School, Auckley

Henry

H enry loves family and friends
E lephants are cute and very big and lovely
N aughty I am not
R ight, Miss Coleman is right, I am not the fastest writer
Y ou have a good friend in me

G ames, rugby is my favourite sport in games
R eading books is my second favourite thing to do
E than is my best friend ever in the world
E xcited as a bee
N ice and kind.

Henry Green (8)
Hill House School, Auckley

Bella Holgate

B eing nice is me
E ntertaining and have great humour
L oving and kind is me
L ove everybody in my family
A nd I love animals

H as a brilliant time doing anything
O wns a dog I love
L ikes all activities
G ood at believing in myself
A m an amazing student
T here's all good things about me
E ncourage myself to have fun.

Bella Holgate (8)
Hill House School, Auckley

This Is Me

I play football and I am as good as Messi

S eagulls are as cheeky as me

A s strong as a dragon

A s tall as a tree

C hloe is my friend

B alls are fun to play with

U p and down the pitch, I run on

R ugby player

T reehouse, my dad made me one in the back garden

O llie is my friend

N othing can stop me from winning my football matches.

Isaac Burton (7)

Hill House School, Auckley

This Is Me

K ind like a dog, but not that kind
A ll the time, I eat cake and sweets
Y ellow is my favourite colour and gold
R hyming is boring, I like acrostics more
A nd games are my life

O zen is my last name, my middle name is Atlas
Z oos are my favourite places to go
E lephants are noisy and I like it
N oisy is my house but I love it because it's my family.

Kayra Ozen (8)
Hill House School, Auckley

This Is Me

T o this day I will always love pizza

H aving a friend cheer me on is all I need

I am a big animal lover and will take care of my dog

S pending time doing sport is my favourite thing

I n the winter I love Christmas dinner

S tudying at school is always fun

M y brother and I love to play football together

E njoying watching Harry Potter is such a treat.

Sophie Bundy (8)

Hill House School, Auckley

This Is Me

T all me can climb tall trees

H ard-working, I work really hard so I feel proud

I mportant because I am a student

S port, I love sport because I like to play football

I am me because I want to be me

S uper, I am super because I like to help my little brother

M anchester United is who I support

E very colour I am unable to see because I am colourblind.

Joshua Pickering (8)

Hill House School, Auckley

Charles

C ool and awesome, that is who I am, this is me.

H ear me, I am me and this is who I want to be.

A mazing me, I'm who I'm meant to be.

R ough but okay, this is who I am and I'll never back down.

L earning is my favourite, I love challenges.

E mbrace who you are and that is who'll you'll stay.

S ee, I don't have friends to help, this is truly who I am.

Omosileola (Charles) Olaniyan (8)

Hill House School, Auckley

All About Elizabeth

E lsie is my nickname, Elizabeth is my fancy name

L ovely Elsie is who I like to be

I love swimming, especially treading water

Z est for life is what I've got

A nimals are always in my heart

B eing with my friends makes me feel happy

E rin is very special to me

T houghtful, kind and caring is the way I was taught to be

H appy is my middle name.

Elizabeth Peacey (6)

Hill House School, Auckley

This Is Jacob

J oking with my friends before the cricket match, high fives all around, celebrating the winning catch

A s autumn leaves fall, back comes the rugby ball

C atching, passing, tackling and scoring, let's see how loud the crowd can start roaring

O n the pitch, I'm in my happy place with anger and determination on my face

B eing me I think is cool because I even have my own swimming pool!

Jacob Mortimore (9)

Hill House School, Auckley

Taliyah

T alented, most definitely she is

A lways dancing, singing, drawing or doing adventurous things

L aughing her head off while smiling for sure

I n glee, she loves jumping and clapping with joy

Y es, I know her as the happiest girl in the world

A mazing as a rockstar performing on stage

H ow wonderful she looks while doing what she loves best.

Taliyah Boyce (7)

Hill House School, Auckley

All About Me

My name is Sienna
I like to sing
But not when the bell goes *ding!*

I want a dog
But my dad says, "No!"
But I say, "Dad, it's not a hog!"

I'm sometimes mad
And maybe silly
But not really sad

I like gardening with my daddy
And baking with my nanna
And shopping with my mummy
This is me.

Sienna Richmond (8)
Hill House School, Auckley

Where Am I?

Pigs, chickens, cows and sheep,
Muddy puddles dotted around,
Sunlight gracefully dancing on the ground,
A place full of life.

Drive around on a big green machine,
Wellies and animals can be seen,
Horses being ridden by the stream,
A place where I'd love to live.

Where am I?

Answer: I am on a farm in the countryside.

Victoria Fitzgibbons (10)
Hill House School, Auckley

This Is Me

T o the study is what I like to do
"H ave a stay at my house," I always say
I like to read but also like to play
S ort of caring for my pets

I have lots of friends
S ort of like dinosaurs

M y school books are really interesting
E ven if I am at school, our pets are cared for.

Penelope Fong (7)
Hill House School, Auckley

Alexander

A lways busy, never tired

L oves every sport except gymnastics

E nergetic and always swimming

X box games are my downtime

A nd family fun is really fun

N ever a day without an activity

D oncaster Dartes is my swimming club

E njoying winning galas, I love them

R eaching my dreams is my goal.

Alex Eggitt (10)

Hill House School, Auckley

This Is Me

T he England football team is my favourite team
H ave lots of football spirit
I love the amazing Man United
S uper friendly, loving to my sister are my adjectives

I am good at football and rugby
S uper worker and very good at maths

M y favourite game is chess
E verybody is my friend!

William Mortimore (7)
Hill House School, Auckley

Harriett

H ello, my name is Harriett and I am honest, helpful and hard-working

A s smart as a cat hunting a hare

R eally kind and caring

R unning and sports aren't my thing

I am a super speedy snake in maths

E veryone loves my cat, Phoebe

T rustworthy, imaginative friend

T hat is the poem all about me.

Harriett Widdowson (9)
Hill House School, Auckley

My Day!

Sometimes, when I go to school
I am not that organised
After all that, I can sit down
And wait for the sophisticated Mr Myatt
His homework is outstanding
It was time for mental maths
And that's when things got really hard
I was hard at work
But then I came across a question
It was too challenging
Will tomorrow be the same?

William Harris (7)

Hill House School, Auckley

Me!

B ig-hearted and kind
E very day, I use my mind
N ice and polite
J essica is my sister, and sometimes we fight
A s happy as a lark
M y favourite time is night, when it's dark
I love pizza and garlic bread for my tea
N ice, nimble, nifty, neat and sometimes naughty.
That's me!

Benjamin Nokes (10)

Hill House School, Auckley

His Name Is...

He travelled to England two times
Destined for greatness and to shine
A player of high expense but worth every penny
The pride is high as he wears the red jersey
As fast as a cheetah, as strong as an ox
With skills and speed
He leaves other players outclassed
The fans all love him wherever he goes
His name is Cristiano Ronaldo.

Oliver Crossley-Fordham (9)
Hill House School, Auckley

Myself

M y favourite sport is hockey, I like to play with my friends

Y ou can often find me singing a lot on the weekend

S ometimes I play basketball at home with my brothers

E ver by myself if I have got no others

L ots of people know that I am a big chatterbox

F orever making friends while wearing spotty socks.

Tara Bluff (10)
Hill House School, Auckley

My Name Is Frankie

F rank the tank is my name

R eading, rhyming is my game

A trip to the park, I love to play

N ear to school is soon I'll stay

K icks ups and cupcakes are all for display

I love to play my favourite, rugby

E very Friday, I do play, I finish with a cheese pizza, that's how I end my day.

Frankie Osborne (5)

Hill House School, Auckley

All About Me!

My name is Giles and I'm nine
I'm a nuisance at home all the time
But when I'm in school
I don't act the fool
The teachers all think I'm divine!

In classes, I'm very polite
And I always get everything right
But once out the gate
The urge is too great
I transform straight back into a tyke!

Giles Highfield (9)
Hill House School, Auckley

The Stables

I feel the breeze
I hear the horses
They whinny as the wind goes by
I see the sky
As bright as the sun
Wondering how life is so good
I ride my horse
Who is as black as the night
And is loving and caring
Looking in the bright sky
I watch the clouds
As I practice my singing
Loving how life is going on.

Scarlett Ross (9)

Hill House School, Auckley

The Rattling Riddle

It is speedy, spotty and sleek
A carnivore with sharp pointy canines
Blend in brilliantly to the African savannah
Extremely speedy
And when it comes to hunting, it is fantastic
The beast has strong legs
Long pointy claws and is a great predator
Sometimes hunts in the day
Sometimes hunts in the night
What am I?

Alexander Drury (8)
Hill House School, Auckley

William

W ingman on the rugby pitch is where I like to be
I adore reading, that is a guarantee
L earning new things is a must for me
L ong bike rides I do enjoy
I am always a smiley, cheerful and happy boy
A nimals, wildlife and farming give me great joy
M y family mean the world to me.

William Hinchliffe (9)

Hill House School, Auckley

This Is Me!

J olly as Santa Claus

A Chinese speaker

Y ellow is my favourite colour

D on't like eggplant as much as I like banana

E very day, I wake up as quick as a shadow

N ut eater

L over of learning from mistakes

E nthusiastic about piano

E xcellent I am!

Jayden Lee (7)
Hill House School, Auckley

It Is Me!

A stronomical at the drums and also likes to play the saxophone.

J ames is one of my best friends and Alex Dickson.

A wesome at laser tag, enjoys playing cricket, football and rugby.

Y our favourite? Mine is a megalodon, it is 65 feet in length and another fact about it is that it has teeth that are five feet.

Ajay Uppal (8)

Hill House School, Auckley

Jorawar Badh

J oy I get from football

O n TV, I watch drums

R unning is fun

A breakdancer

W ater is my dog's name

A mong Us player

R ugby player

B ooks I like to read

A superstar I am

D ancing around my room

H aving so much fun.

Jorawar Badh (7)

Hill House School, Auckley

Ethan Jones

E than is my name and I am a pizza lover
T oo much chocolate eater
H elpful to my friends
A bird watcher
N ot a bad guitar player

J olly and joyful
O nwards biker
N ot a bad badminton player
E xcellent exerciser
S uper good helper.

Ethan Jones (7)
Hill House School, Auckley

Annabelle

A m a lover of beautiful things
N eat as I can possibly be
N aughty, that's not me
A mazing at dancing
B right as a light
E very day, I try my best
L ovely at the piano
L ove to play with my sister
E ntertaining my sister, that's what I like.

Annabelle Brown (7)
Hill House School, Auckley

I Am George

I love my dog, Winnie

A mazing super ninja spy
M y cosy bed makes me happy

G reat at Lego building
E verybody loves to play with me
O utgoing and a chatterbox
R eally good at giving hugs
G oal scoring king
E xcellent piano player.

George Christian (6)
Hill House School, Auckley

This Is Me

T all as a giraffe
H appy as a bee
I ntelligent as a book
S ometimes I can be silly

I am me and you are you
S ometimes, I can get extremely excited

M aybe I could get better at reading
E nd of lessons, I do not like.

Arya Basra (8)
Hill House School, Auckley

A Boy Called Charlie

There once was a boy called Charlie
Who had a friend called Marley
From Monday to Sunday, they loved to play
And never would miss a day
Bumps and scrapes all around
But no other passion had they found
As many times as they were shoved
Football was the game Charlie truly loved.

Charlie Stanley (9)
Hill House School, Auckley

Animals

A nimals are amazing, adventurous creatures
N ever nip you
I nsects make you itchy
M aggie the magpie flew to Mexico
A n ant was eating an apple
L uca the lizard ate a lemon from a tree
S ally the starfish was selling seawater on the sand.

Mila Curtis (11)

Hill House School, Auckley

Ballerina Princess

L ovely and kind
Y ear one superstar
D og lover
I ce cream muncher
A lways helpful

G reat swimmer
O ften cheeky
D reaming of princesses
L ikes to dance
E ats all the sweets
Y our friend.

Lydia Godley (5)
Hill House School, Auckley

Football Mad

J oyful and smiley when I play football

O ver the summer, I loved to play football

S uper at scoring goals

H appiest with a ball at my feet

U nderstanding more about football after every training session

A fter I score a goal, I run down the pitch.

Joshua Price-Stephens (6)

Hill House School, Auckley

Xander

X marks the spot of the secret mark between my toes

A nkylosaurus is one of my favourite dinos

N inja is my hobby

D ragons are my favourite too

E veryone knows I like the Hungry Hippo game

R ichmond is my last name and my eyes are coloured blue.

Xander Richmond (5)

Hill House School, Auckley

The Hare

The hare sat there
With a grin on his face
It is the time and place
Autumn is now the case
The leaves will turn red
Like the old grandma said
And the people will rise from the dead
You can jump in the leaves
And climb the trees
It's the season of Halloween.

Caitlyn Gibson (8)
Hill House School, Auckley

Tobias

T obias is my name, but everyone calls me Toby
O bey the rules of the school
B rave when I get a graze
I nterested in pigeons and fast cars
A cting is my thing, I am a drama king
S uperpowers I have a few, to take care of the new boys at school.

Tobias Hodgson (6)

Hill House School, Auckley

Thomas

T rying hard is what I like to do

H aving lots of fun with my friends

O utside playing sport and farming are my favourite

M y heart is always warm and loving

A nimals make me very happy every day

S miles are the best gifts I give to my family.

Thomas Hinchliffe (6)

Hill House School, Auckley

All About Me

C razy, I'm helpful

A nd I'm happy all the time

S o playful and hard-working

S o happy and pleased that I go to school and make friends

I hate flies, they tickle you like animals licking you

E nd of the day, time to go skateboarding.

Cassie Hather (7)

Hill House School, Auckley

Daisy

This Daisy was born in 1983
A very special flower to my family and me
This Daisy is a symbol of dying love
It had lost all its petals
That was sent from above
If I can nurse it back to life
Unlock its soul with a key
Will you, Daisy
Come back again to my family?

Dora Mayil (9)
Hill House School, Auckley

This Is Me!

A kennings poem

I am a...
Fast reader
Animal lover
Flower collector
Sweet eater
Ice lolly lover
Hockey player
Hockey watcher
Christmas lover
Song writer
Shell collector
Roblox lover
Light sleeper
Not hater
Good helper.

Romie Fletcher (7)
Hill House School, Auckley

Edward

E very day, I like to play football

D oes like playing outdoors

W illing to help anyone out

A lways likes dressing as Batman

R eally good at baking cakes

D oesn't like getting washed or putting suncream on.

Edward Gregory (6)

Hill House School, Auckley

This Is Me

T aekwondo star
H istory hooligan
I ncredible book reader
S uper at football

I ncredible rugby player
S uper sweet eater

M arvellous mathematician
E xcited piano player.

Finley Christian (7)
Hill House School, Auckley

Pashley

P onies, I love to ride ponies
A nimals, I love animals
S ophie is my middle name
H ating animals is no good
L oving animals is what I do
E lla Pashley is my name
Y ou and me are all different.

Ella Pashley (8)
Hill House School, Auckley

This Is Me!

A kennings poem

I am a...
Pizza eater
Hip-hop dancer
Football player
Good baker
Drum player
Chocolate eater
Pasta eater
Languages speaker
Football watcher
Building person
Hockey player
Throwing catcher
Sweet eater.

Eliza Ardron-Levack (8)
Hill House School, Auckley

Farmer Jones

J olly little farmer
E ggs are my favourite thing
N ever forgetting Barty
S ix chickens I have got
O nly two little ducks though. *Quack! Quack!*
N ever a quiet moment on Jolly Jenson's farm.

Jenson Jones (5)
Hill House School, Auckley

Bon Bon Delight

Take two spoonfuls of kindness
A cup of generosity
A sprinkle of drama
And some caring, sharing extra daring cleverness
Then into the oven for a little warmth
Before taking out and decorating with glitz
This is the best Bon Bon mix!

Bronwyn Jones (9)
Hill House School, Auckley

Popcorn

Popcorn is yellow
It sounds like secrets being revealed
It feels like a tasty treat I've been waiting for
It smells like a burning fire
It tastes like a cheerful sweet feeling inside of me
I know this will make my mood a lot better.

Omosede Izehor (9)
Hill House School, Auckley

You'll Be There By Noon

Everything I do
I do it like you
Stretch to the moon
You'll be there soon

Like a star
Going to Mars
With a tap and a point
And gymnastics bar

Don't blink too soon
You'll be there by noon.

Annabelle Layden (9)
Hill House School, Auckley

All About Me!

A kennings poem

I am a...
Good baker
Rabbit lover
Music player
Book reader
Good dancer
Brilliant singer
Movie watcher
Halloween enjoyer
Chocolate eater
Late sleeper
Pizza maker
Friend hugger
Excellent helper.

Arya Luniya (8)
Hill House School, Auckley

Nature And Me

Mrs Ladybird walked up to me
And she had a wee
Mrs Butterfly was colourful
And I think she is wonderful
Mr Caterpillar was fluffy
Around his tummy
I like little nature
And little nature likes me,
Because we are free!

Esraa Wragg (5)
Hill House School, Auckley

Matilda

M y hair is orange and curly
A lways happy and kind
T alks and laughs a lot
I s amazing at swimming
L oves to eat sweets
D ancing is so fun for me
A lways helpful and always tidy.

Matilda Hoad (6)

Hill House School, Auckley

This Is Me!

A kennings poem

I am a...
Fantastic swimmer
Sweety eater
Late riser
Great footballer
Autumn wisher
Chocolate buns maker
Deep sleeper
Bug fleer
Animal lover
TV watcher
Aeroplane watcher
Smarties swallower.

Seth Markham
Hill House School, Auckley

Emily

E liza is my beautiful little sister

M aybe I will be a doctor when I grow up

I love dancing ballet because I wear pretty clothes

L oves to be a purple princess

Y o-yo Bears are my favourite snack.

Emily Brannan (6)

Hill House School, Auckley

Robin Ray, This Is Robin

R eally nice and kind
O ften is funny
B rilliant at skating
I s dreaming of the Olympics
N ot bad at cooking

R eally helpful
A t home
Y ay! That's Robin!

Robin Peirce (6)
Hill House School, Auckley

This Is Me!

A kennings poem

I am a...
Football fan
Sweet eater
Early riser
Great gymnast
Helpful girl
Friend maker
Pet owner
Caring sister
Neat writer
Amazing girl
Orange lover
Star watcher
Magic Tiles player.

Sophia Clarkson (7)
Hill House School, Auckley

Islands

T his is me
H as facts about
I slands
S ometimes

I slands that are unusual and unique
S ometimes made of snakes

M ight be really unusual
E ven scary.

Ebony Dent (10)
Hill House School, Auckley

This Is Me

A kennings poem

I am a...
Book reader
Great baker
Good helper
Piano player
Tennis player
Pizza eater
Crab hunter
Amazing biker
Roblox player
Great runner
Hockey player
Recorder player
Pasta eater.

Amelia Drury (7)
Hill House School, Auckley

This Is Me

A kennings poem

This is me...
Chocolate eater
Sweet eater
Book reader
Football player
Rugby player
Present opener
Cricket player
Homework lover
Cat lover
Drawing fan
Fortnite player
School lover.

Oliver Pickering (7)

Hill House School, Auckley

This Is Me

I like to have fun with my little dog
He likes to jump as high as he wants
He likes to eat his food
But he is very greedy
He gobbles it down
He likes to eat anything
He is so cute
What type of dog is he?

Lucy Barker (9)
Hill House School, Auckley

My Favourite Animal Is?

It has black skin
Head as hard as an iron tin
Its pups learn
It dives and makes the water churn
It wears a coat of transparent fur
It dances across the Arctic
Terroriser of seals
Murderer of albatrosses.

Sebastian Aylmer (9)
Hill House School, Auckley

Vivaan

V ery fun to have and to play with
I maginative to myself and my house
V ery good for my house
A lways hard-working
A lways happy
N imble student and cool, this is me!

Vivaan Bhounsle (8)
Hill House School, Auckley

This Is Me

Super sporty, speedy
Theo is fast
He won't be last
Great going gangbees
Gaming is fun
You will never miss out on gaming
Happy, delirious, having fun
Likes to play cricket in the sun.

Theo Millington (10)
Hill House School, Auckley

This Is Me

A kennings poem

I am a...
Harry fan
Book reader
Hockey player
Pizza eater
Dog lover
TV watcher
Bike rider
Sweet eater
Friend maker
School lover
Tennis player
Taekwondo starter.

Sarah Mirza (7)
Hill House School, Auckley

Super Robyn

R eally curly hair
O ver the top bossy because I really care
B est brothers ever
Y es, I'm really clever
N othing compares to sucking my fingers and tapping my hair.

Robyn Close (5)

Hill House School, Auckley

How To Make A Reuben

To make a Reuben, you will need:
Two cups of kindness and a bucket of love
Next, add a hat full of clever
Stir in some smiles and a pinch of luck
Bake in the oven for 100 seconds
Kiss to taste.

Reuben Bennett (5)
Hill House School, Auckley

Willow

W illow is wonderful
I ntelligent and kind
L oving and caring
L et's bear that in mind
O utrageously funny as you can see
W illow is wise and she is me!

Willow Powell (9)

Hill House School, Auckley

Everyone's Friend

I nterested in everything

S miley and always happy

A mazing in every way

B right as a morning

E veryone's friend

L istens and cares for everyone.

Isabel Price-Stephens (6)

Hill House School, Auckley

This Is Me!

A kennings poem

I am a...
Distance runner
Fast learner
Tennis player
Deep sleeper
Chocolate eater
Good helper
Piano player
Great brother
Mum helper
Bike rider
Car washer.

Moses Ilori (7)
Hill House School, Auckley

Ayesha

A yesha loves chocolate
Y es, it's true
E ggs, bars and Smarties
S he will share them too
H er favourite is caramel
A nd Chocolate Orange.

Ayesha Thomas (6)
Hill House School, Auckley

This Is Me!

A kennings poem

I am a...
Football lover
Fantastic reader
Excellent speller
Love summer
Fast runner
Amazing goalkeeper
Multiplication hero
Love school
Fantastic gamer.

Henry Burkitt (7)

Hill House School, Auckley

Nahla

N ever have I not been kind
A ll my friends are kind
H ave I been a good student
L ollipops are my favourite sweet
A dam is my big brother.

Nahla Walton (6)
Hill House School, Auckley

What Is It...?

A fluffy pet
Cute and as fast
As a bolt of lightning
Amazing bird killer
Long whiskers
Fluffy coat
Great mouse catcher
What am I?

I am a cat.

Felix Cameron (8)
Hill House School, Auckley

Adhya As I Am!

A lways being kind and helpful

D oes things right

H as a unique style

Y ou can trust me as a friend

A crobatics is my favourite sport.

Adhya Chandra (6)

Hill House School, Auckley

Henry

H elpful and kind
E xcited for every playtime
N eat writing every day
R eady for Ruggereds
Y ummy chocolate is my favourite.

Henry Barlow (5)

Hill House School, Auckley

About Me

M any talents he's got
I s a very friendly boy
C an run fast
A clever boy he is
H e likes to play with dinosaurs.

Micah Luhanga (5)

Hill House School, Auckley

This Is Me!

A kennings poem

I am a...
Book reader
Bee fleer
Football watcher
Chocolate eater
Football player
Early riser
SuperThing collector
Maths lover.

Noah Otley (7)
Hill House School, Auckley

This Is Me

A kennings poem

Game gamer
Football player
Rugby player
Bike rider
Smart student

Dog walker
Farmer lover
Poppit collector
Sweet eater.

Dexter Hewson (7)

Hill House School, Auckley

This Is Me!

A kennings poem

I am a...
Good reader
Fast runner
Football watcher
Fast eater
Sweet eater
Deep sleeper
Late riser
Dog walker
Dog owner.

Louis Jesson (7)
Hill House School, Auckley

Me

A kennings poem

Book reader
Singing teacher
Book writer
Apple collector
Wasp catcher
Sugar eater
Light sleeper
Poppit sharer
Movie watcher.

Sophia Dudgeon (7)
Hill House School, Auckley

This Is Me

A kennings poem

I am a...
Horse rider
Sugar monster
Dresser upper
Hard worker
Deep sleeper
Gingerbread maker
Dog owner
Amazing singer.

Emily Blunt (7)

Hill House School, Auckley

This Is Me

A kennings poem

Horse rider
Book reader
Pole vaulter
Amazing singer
Dog walker
Devoted sister
Animal lover
Family member
Baby lover.

Bella Damary-Wilson (7)
Hill House School, Auckley

Ayda's Song

A wesome is what she is
Y es, she actually is
D id you know about it?
A yda loves singing.

Ayda Davallo (6)
Hill House School, Auckley

I Am Me

I don't like dresses, I like sports
I like to be comfy, but I don't like shorts

My hair is curly, sometimes it doesn't behave
No matter how hard I try, it always looks insane!

I'm not like my sister, even though we're
both smart
She's into make-up, but I'm into art

I am happy the way I am and I am blessed to be
Different and an individual, I am me.

Amelia Miah (9)
Lawrence Community Primary School, Wavertree

How To Make Me!

If you want to know how to make me
Then follow me and you will see
Put your apron on
And let's start baking
And I'm telling you
This will be worth making
Add some sugar
Both brown and white
And mix it up with all your might
Add three eggs
And butter too
And mix it up like a witch's brew
Add vanilla extract
Salt as well
That should give it a delightful smell
Sift some flour
And add it in
Then add some milk
That will make it nice and thin
Pour it into a cake tin
And let it set

Now it's done
Hmm... this isn't complete yet
Now let's cover it in frosting
And make it all smooth
Let's cover the sides in sprinkles too
Let's put some icing into a piping bag
Now let's squeeze it out
It looks totally rad!

Maisha Miah (9)
Lawrence Community Primary School, Wavertree

This Is Me, Lexie!

L exie is lovely and likeable

E nergetic, excellent and exciting, dancing is my favourite hobby

X mas spent at Granny and Grandad's

I love it!

E njoys playing with Barbies with my sister, Tilda.

L ego building is a lot of fun

O ctober is my birthday month

V ery cute doggies make my jaw drop

E ating peas is yuck!

S haun the Sheep is my favourite teddy.

A dventurous, amazing animal lover

N othing can stop me stroking my Granny and Grandad's pet dog, Spider

I maginary unicorns are real

M y best friends are Charlotte and Freya

A ll I want is a dog of my own

L exie has glasses, golden hair and greeny-brown eyes

S nuggly Snowy is my pet rabbit.

Lexie Bechman (8)

Mary Exton Primary School, Hitchin

This Is Me, Tilda!

I am a tall, green-eyed girl with chestnut-brown
curly hair,
Kind-hearted, friendly and loyal, I want life
to be fair.

Adventurous, brave, funny and compassionate,
Sushi is something I really hate!

I love to go on holiday and swim in the shimmering
sapphire pool,
My favourite things are reading books and
learning maths when I go to school.

Dancing is a hobby of mine, it's really a lot of fun,
I like building sandcastles on the beach and eating
ice cream in the sun.

Sumer is my black pet rabbit,
I like riding my bike and bouncing on the
trampoline to keep fit.

Listening to funky pop music makes me
want to sing,
Cuddling fluffy, playful pandas would be a
wonderful thing!

Tilda Bechman (10)
Mary Exton Primary School, Hitchin

Me, Myself And I

Grace is my name
I love candy canes
I am ten
I have seen Big Ben
I am a female
I want to see a whale
I measure 126
And I love to eat Twix
My hair is a chocolate brown
I wish I had a gold crown
I have forever eyes
I love my dad's pies
I have been to Alton Towers
I would love superpowers
I love to eat
I'm not very neat
I am very jolly
I have a friend called Molly
Emma is my friend

I know why bananas bend
My daddy is so cool
He always acts the fool.

Grace Degnan-Gordon (10)

Mary Exton Primary School, Hitchin

This Is Me, Aaryahi!

I love maths, English and PE,
Because they have fun activities!

I love jumping on my bouncy trampoline,
And swinging on my new swing.
On a cold, rainy day,
I love playing chess with my dad!

I love when it is our turn,
To go on the climbing frame,
It is as fun as going down a slippery slide!
I talk sweetly to everyone I meet,
I am as friendly as a capybara!

I'd like to see a greener world,
Where everyone could breathe easy.

Aaryahi Pathak (7)
Mary Exton Primary School, Hitchin

Me And Dyslexia

D yslexia is hard but with help, okay

Y ou are good in your own way

S pellings I find hard but stupid I am not

L anguages, science and music I like a lot

E xtra things like coloured paper and overlays really help

X -rays can't show dyslexia, it's not something you see

I don't like dyslexia as I find school hard, but will work harder so I can be

A n astronaut or scientist because that's what interests me.

Ivy Knowles (9)

Mary Exton Primary School, Hitchin

The Recipe Of Me

A scoopful of happiness
A drop full of love
A teardrop of sadness
Mix it up clockwise
Add two tablespoons of laughter
A bust of friendship
Two teaspoons of fun
Cut up the bravery
Stir counter-clockwise
Half a bottle of kindness
A tablespoon of honesty
A teaspoon of anger
A dash of rights
A squirt of positivity
A dash of creativity
Preheat the oven to seven years old
Leave for five months
And then you'll have me!

Evelyn Wilcox (7)
Mary Exton Primary School, Hitchin

All About Me

Not many people seem to know
That my happiness starts to flow
My hair's so curly, it even glows
No, I want my hair short
I don't want it to grow
When I was a baby
My favourite colour was yellow
Now I like to sit in front of the fire
and eat marshmallows
Our school words are inspirational,
creative and caring
In our school, we are always laughing and sharing
I have a few friends and I wanted to tell you
This is me!

Isla Skeggs (10)

Mary Exton Primary School, Hitchin

Why I Like Foxes

I like foxes because they're cute
I like foxes because of their red and orange suit
Foxes can run at the most amazing speed
Almost as fast as a humble old steed
I like foxes because they're soft
Definitely as soft as the fluff in the loft
I like foxes because they burrow underground
Far deeper than a hunter's hound
This is me, a girl who likes foxes
I prefer them in fields rather than boxes.

Daisy Buckridge (8)
Mary Exton Primary School, Hitchin

Big Sister, Bella

My name is Bella
I have a baby brother
He's a cute little fella

He likes to call me mummy
Which I find really funny

Sometimes I help my mum
And change his stinky bum

When he has a clean nappy
He is much more happy

He loves to have a bath
And makes us all laugh

Me and Gerry were both born at the Lister
And I'm so proud to be his big sister!

Isabella Boyle (8)
Mary Exton Primary School, Hitchin

1,000 Years Ago

Did cavemen ride on dinosaurs?
Did pixies live in the snow?
Did fiction books tell the truth
1,000 years ago?

Did unicorns rule the world?
Did fish live on land?
Did row boats even row
1,000 years ago?

Did people even read?
Did people go to school?
How far did people go
1,000 years ago?

Bryony Hall (10)
Mary Exton Primary School, Hitchin

I Like This

I am Trixie
This is me
I love horses
And tomato sauces
I own a fluffy bunny
Who eats cardboard which is funny
I watch movies starring unicorns
While eating bowls of sweet popcorn
I'm good at doing gymnastics
My cartwheels are fantastics
My BFF is called Evie
These are the things that make Trixie!

Beatrix Hyde (7)
Mary Exton Primary School, Hitchin

Lucie Is Me

L ucie, that's me
U nbelievable horse rider
C ool kid
I mpatient at times
E xcited to learn

R eally reading ready
A mazing artist
Y ay! I am me
N ever seen a rhino at a zoo
E lephants are my favourite zoo animal
R hia is my BFF.

Lucie Rayner (9)
Mary Exton Primary School, Hitchin

Lexie

My name is Lexie
I do not like Pepsi
I love to do art
I have a big heart
I like sweets
I also like the ancient Greeks

I always try to be kind
I always follow the saying 'no man left behind'
My personality is energetic
I like to think of myself as empathetic
This is me.

Lexie Marie Copp (9)
Mary Exton Primary School, Hitchin

My Family

Claire is a chatterbox,
Big Charlie is tall,
Grandma likes spending her money,
Mum likes drinking coffee,
Grampy has a nice cat,
Meg has a lot of energy,
Macie is a TikToker,
Aaron likes wearing jeans,
Amy is crazy like her twin, Meg,
Luna is nice and fluffy.

Charlie Carrick (7)
Mary Exton Primary School, Hitchin

This Is Me

I like sports,
I like all sorts,
I like gaming,
I like it when it's raining,

I am funny,
I am silly,
I am friendly,
I am happy,

I like pizza,
I like pasta,
I like tigers,
But most of all,
I love my little sister.

Olly Backhouse (7)
Mary Exton Primary School, Hitchin

I Wish...

I wish I could fly
And soar up into the sky

Sometimes I wish
That I had a fish

I wish I had powers
One about flowers

But my most important wish
One more important than any fish

Is to be
Just like me!

Emma Sanchez Andreu (9)
Mary Exton Primary School, Hitchin

Annabel

A wesome family

N ever gives up

N ow type one diabetic

A lways kind and helpful

B ella-Rose is my best friend

E xceptionally brave

L ittle sister is Poppy.

Annabel Davies (9)

Mary Exton Primary School, Hitchin

My Favourite Things

M y favourite subject is maths

A dding is lots of fun

T aking away needs help from my mum

H appy singing and dancing I am

S wimming like a mermaid is something I can do.

Freya Knowles (7)

Mary Exton Primary School, Hitchin

Rhia

R ight now, I am nine
H aving ballet lessons every Thursday
I like spending time with my friends and family
A nd my birthday is on the 5th of October.

Rhia Mather-Howard (9)
Mary Exton Primary School, Hitchin

All About Me

Of all the children in the school
I might not be the tallest
And definitely not a genius
I might not know how to spell well
And create an enchanting story

But I am a role model to others and valued
Listen to and heard by my fellow classmates

Of all the people in my house
I might not be the most ambitious
And get all the marks on my paper
I might not have a good report
And some days not be happy

But I have a warm loving family that loves
me for everything
That cherish every moment we have together

Of all the people in the world
I might not be the most renowned
And don't have a million friends

I might not be the best at maths
And be the most sympathetic person

But I have a voice that people hear
have shelter and food with an awesome family
And I can't ask for anything more as I have
everything that I need
And I will treat others respectfully.

Alicja Targos (10)
Our Lady's Catholic Primary School, Dartford

As Humble As A Bumblebee

Striving to forgive instead of hating
I love all subjects like writing and artistic creating
To bring joy and fun, filling everyone with glee
As humble as a bumblebee

Liking many different hues of colours
From midnight black to cotton white and
many others
Eating grapes to strawberries, broccoli to peas
Meat to seafood, from land to sea

I like to sing and dance
To the magnificent music of K-pop bands
Baking, cooking, swimming, making good deeds
Becoming a good citizen, to help everyone in
their needs

Socialising with family and friends
Loving the fun that I wish never ends
I'd like to fly like bees for the world I'd love to see
As humble as a bumblebee

My heart always beats with love
To promote peace like a delightful dove
As humble as a bee I want everyone to be
This is me!

Nathaniel Salazar (11)

Our Lady's Catholic Primary School, Dartford

The Recipe To Being Me!

First of all, you'll need a cup of humour,
To brighten up any touch of anger, displeasure
or hostility,
Which is such a pleasure!
Next, you'll need a touch of curiosity,
So that all my questions will be answered
immediately like a cheetah you see.
Furthermore, add a pinch of agitation like
thunderous storms above the surface of the sea.
Then add a cup of intelligence,
As I study which makes me very smart and helps
my future as far as clouds in the distance.
Within a second, add half a spoonful of
forgiveness,
So I can spread peace to the world,
Which leads us to the next verse.
Later on, add double a cup of peace,
To brighten up our world perfectly.
Afterwards, add a cup of ferociousness,
So I can fight off any predators.
Lastly, add a bowl of awesomeness so I can fly
and be me!

Oreoluwa Olawoye (10)
Our Lady's Catholic Primary School, Dartford

What Should I Be?

Should I be a robust carpenter whose schedule's
always busy
Or should I be a judge searching for the innocent
and guilty
I'm adamant I could be a jubilant nursery teacher
I could also be a pastor, a praying preacher
My aspirations and dreams can be really hard
to find
But one day I'll find my path and way
I love to speak and write, I'm a linguistic poet
People laugh and jeer, even stare but for me, I
could never care
I love to have the tenacity
Love, sereneness, kindness and generosity
I like to shine as bright as the sun
I will endure the challenges
Because there is no gain without pain!

Nifemi Omisade (10)
Our Lady's Catholic Primary School, Dartford

All About Me

H ello, my name is Courtney
I rely on my sunny attitude to support me

M y loving Nigerian culture
Y ells at me to make a sculpture

N ice and warm as the sunshine
A rt and music is all mine
M y passion for sports is amazing
E dward and Jasmine, my sibling, in sports are raising

I give people crafts I make
S uch as a drawing of a birthday cake

C reativity calls my name
O verall, that is my aim
U nder all of it is writing too
R eading is what I like to do

T eaching people the importance of art

N ando's, my favourite restaurant, recipe for me is yummy and smart

E nding this lovely poem all about me

Y ou have learnt one or two things about me you see.

Courtney Anyaegbuna (10)

Our Lady's Catholic Primary School, Dartford

What I Like And My Life

My name is Marcus and I'd like to say
That right now, I am nine today
If you want to know more about me
Then in the poem, you shall see
My favourite game is basketball
I love that game and that's for sure
I like eating rice and pizza too
I love my family and that is 100% true
I finish my homework sometimes on time
Just keep going, I can't think of a rhyme
I use my laptop and my phone
I love ice cream and ice cream cones
At bedtime, my brother likes a bedtime story
At bedtime, I sometimes have a cup of tea
What I like and what I see, is my friends and family.

Marcus Lawal (9)
Our Lady's Catholic Primary School, Dartford

Things About Me

This poem is all about me
I assume it is quite clear to see
I have a brother who is the youngest of us all
Especially younger than me who is not very tall
You might not know, but I am fond of
manga books
I am also into the food my mum cooks
Things I like to watch are anime
I also communicate with my friends almost
every day.

Kaycee Cassandra Duenas (10)
Our Lady's Catholic Primary School, Dartford

That's My Name!

S tays positive at all times

A lways knows what to do when people tell white lies

N ever lets her friends stay upset

T ells people what to do when they forget

Y ells at people sometimes but not on purpose

O ccasionally dances like she is part of a circus.

Santy Ofosu-Asamoah (10)
Our Lady's Catholic Primary School, Dartford

This Is Me

T all and strong
H appy and grateful
I ndependent
S mart as a lightbulb

I ntelligent
S ix is my brother's age

M essy and disorganised
E mpathy to others.

Azoma Egeruka (9)
Our Lady's Catholic Primary School, Dartford

Things I Love And Me

I love cats and black caps
My family, I love the most
Rose, Joseph and Rapie
And all the people I love as well
My personality is passionate and kind
I'm very shy most of the time
I'm by myself but it's my time to shine
My dream is to meet my stepsister
Her name is Ruby
Shining like a crystal
When I'm happy, I love to make people smile
But when I'm crying, it's just for a while
This me, can't you see?
I love to care and share
The ones I care about
Are my teachers, friends and family
I always think that my friendship and life
will never end
My life is quite amazing
I know that's true
My brown hair waves and twists in the air

My eyes glow in the dark like a cat and
look like the sea
My life is so mysterious, can't you see?
This is me!

Audrey Serafin (8)
Ruislip Gardens Primary School, Ruislip

The Ingredients To Make Me

To create me, you will need:
A bowl of sprinkled cupcakes
1,000 cats
10,000 unicorns with rainbow wings
A dash of happiness
Ten candy canes
A pinch of James and the Giant Peach
A world full of girls
A pool full of loving puppies

Now you need to:
Add a bowl of sprinkled cupcakes and
loving puppies
Mix in a lot of cats and unicorns
Stir roughly while adding ten candy canes
And a dash of happiness
Next, add a pinch of giant peach
Then spread neatly over a tray of baking paper

Cook until glazed and fun-filled bubbles can
be seen
Sprinkle on some more candy canes and leave
to cool down
This is me!

Bleu Cass (8)
Ruislip Gardens Primary School, Ruislip

This Is Me!

This is all the ingredients you'll need:
A dash of fun
A pinch of sweet
A mix of cakes and sweets
A lifetime of football, also lots of goals
And don't forget, I am as fast as a cheetah

Now you need to:
Put the pinch of sweet in the bowl
Next, add a dash of fun in there too
A lifetime of football and don't forget the goals
Crumbly cakes and sugary sweets, that would be nice
And don't forget I'm as fast as a cheetah, add some of that too
Now mix it for twenty minutes or more
Wait until pretty, just like me
Take it out, add some sugary sprinkles
Eat it and it will taste just like me
This is me!

Bella-Rose Rogers (8)
Ruislip Gardens Primary School, Ruislip

This Is Me!

Two teaspoons of laughter
A pinch of snoozing, snoring sleep
A dollop of disaster
A sprinkle of my alarm clock going *beep!*
A dash of dancing
A slab of pasta
A spoon of prancing
And I am the master

Add two teaspoons of laughter
And some snoozing, snoring sleep
But make sure you add a dollop of disaster
Stir as fast as a roundabout
Some sprinkles of my alarm clock going *beep!*
Add a dash of dancing
Mix all the ingredients
Some slabs of pasta
And I am the master
This is me!

Erin Carter (8)
Ruislip Gardens Primary School, Ruislip

All About Me

T oday I'm happy and you can see

H ome is the best place I have ever been

I always love playing radical Roblox and marvellous Minecraft

S mile and come along with me, so you can see

I love mischievous meerkats, they're so cute indeed

S o everything I told you is so true

M y family are the best people ever, I love them so much

E verybody knows I love chocolate so come along with me and you can see that I am Freya and... this is me!

Freya Lucia Patel (8)

Ruislip Gardens Primary School, Ruislip

Animal Lover

T his is me, an animal lover

H ere and now, no matter what animal, I will always love them

I don't care if it bites, as long as it's happy, I'm happy

S o that means I'm an animal lover, I guess

I don't care what people say about animals, I know they're good

S o no matter what, I will always love animals

M e and animals will be together forever and ever

E veryone should love animals as long as animals love them.

Mia Manning (8)

Ruislip Gardens Primary School, Ruislip

The Things I Love

T here's a sport called football that I love

H e's a superstar in boots, surely quicker than a dove

I nspiration was the key

S eeing the reality

I love cheetahs so much

S ea creatures aren't bad too

M eeting my friends I do so love, they give me encouragement here and there

E ven though they don't have time to spare.

Antony Caron (8)
Ruislip Gardens Primary School, Ruislip

Recipe For Me!

First, you should:
Grab a pair of pans
Next, get some swimming eggs from the
Wonderful colourful fridge
Then add a pinch of smart sugar
And a sprinkle of respectful rice
With a splash of thrilling krill
And a dash of fearful saltiness

Now mix all the noble alphabets
And leave it to cool down
And then you will be so surprised your
head will explode.

Danii Reguretsky (8)
Ruislip Gardens Primary School, Ruislip

This Is Me

T his is me, I like football
H ave you ever seen a cool 360?
I have done a lot of super cool dribbles
S o, I will train for a month

I know I lost some matches
S ome super cool dribbles I can't do

M y dad helps me with my football
E very day, I train with my dad for my football club.

Eduardo Martins Aguiar (8)

Ruislip Gardens Primary School, Ruislip

How To Make Me

To create me, you need:
50x craziness
50x mischief
20x friendship
Some princess, fashion and gaming items
A few of my favourite sweets
A bunch of toys
Three brothers
And a dash of glitter and brightness

All you need to do now is:
Put them all in the pot
Now, look at what you made...
You made the best creature ever!

Ashlee Doorga (8)
Ruislip Gardens Primary School, Ruislip

This Is Me!

To create me, you will need:
A puzzle-filled room
A wedge of juicy burger
10lb of mischief and fun
A pinch of drama
A dash of cheekiness
A sprinkle of sadness

Now you need to:
Add a dash of cheekiness
A sprinkle of sadness
A pinch of drama
A puzzle-filled room
A wedge of juicy burger.

Summer Gambell (8)
Ruislip Gardens Primary School, Ruislip

This Is Me

I am a...
Cat lady
Chocolate eater
Robux begger
Dad's chicken lover
Wasp fleer
Annoying sister
Large-tempered person
Not a very calm girl
Loud-voiced human
Big-brained sister
As slow as a potato
Roblox addict
I shout so loud I will lose my voice
Lastly, a pizza lover.

Fallon Hewitt (8)
Ruislip Gardens Primary School, Ruislip

My Rap

I am helpful and kind
I am a useful guy
I am a clever guy
And I am a bit shy
But I always say hi
And I will never cry
But I love to lie
I never say bye
But don't worry
When I don't say bye
I am kind
Because I am a useful
Understanding
Appreciative guy
This is me.

Hugo Bwalya (8)
Ruislip Gardens Primary School, Ruislip

Me

T he dancing I do makes me happy
H eading out to swim is fun
I t is the thing that I learn
S ee, I love to sing and dance

I see music as a sight
S ince I was little, I loved to sing

M y room was my dancefloor
E legant dancer, fabulous actress.

Ruby Freeman (9)
Ruislip Gardens Primary School, Ruislip

This Is Me

T alented dancer, twirling and swirling
H air is as blonde as the sun
I n the blink of an eye, I am here to help
S mile as shiny as a diamond

I rresitible smile
S uperstar singer

M ighty, amazing teacher
E lephant lover.

Peyia McCarville (8)
Ruislip Gardens Primary School, Ruislip

My Things

I read through books as fast as a cheetah
I swim at supersonic speed
Omelette makes me go down
But chocolate makes me go, "Whee! Yummy!"
I absolutely love brown bears and
elegant elephants
They're fluffy and friendly
My friends are always there for me
This is me.

Matilda Cotton (9)

Ruislip Gardens Primary School, Ruislip

This Is Me

T he helpful parrot
H e is as kind as a husky
I can make dog, cat and wolf sounds
S o I can be them and be their friend

I can be responsible
S o I am kind

M y heart is on fire
E xcited to be here.

Joseph Leach (8)
Ruislip Gardens Primary School, Ruislip

My Ordinary Life

I am...
Animal lover
Terrified to hover
Game liker
Soon to be hiker
Love a snowy Saturday
Least favourite animal is a joey
Really fast like Albert Einstein
Needs more pets
Rugby is the best game
Not lovely when I've got to go to a club.

Joud Hobi (8)
Ruislip Gardens Primary School, Ruislip

All About My Life

There's a sport called rugby
That I really love
It's my favourite sport
My love for my family
Is as big as my heart

I come from Africa
It is famous for their animals
Every rugby player has a team
My dad supports the Cheetahs.

Aiden Smit (8)
Ruislip Gardens Primary School, Ruislip

Who Am I?

I want to be loved
My favourite food is pizza
I like to sing like a star
To calm myself, I like to write like an author
I love school because of maths
Also because of Miss Keene, I learn
Also, I get to see my BFF
Who am I?

Whaj Al Karam (8)
Ruislip Gardens Primary School, Ruislip

This Is Me

T iny

H air as gold as the shining sun

I rresistible smile

S wimmer without goggles

I ce cream lover

S uper singer

M aths is so fun

E xcellent egg eater.

Tilly Rose Evans (8)

Ruislip Gardens Primary School, Ruislip

This Is Me!

T oday, I am happy
H appy I am
I love to sing
S inging sweetly

I love my teacher
S he is sweet

M aria is me
E veryone knows that I love cakes.

Maria Frankie (9)
Ruislip Gardens Primary School, Ruislip

Potion Of Mine

To be my BFF you will need...
A dash of smiles
And some faith
A lot of caring
A bit of strong
And a bit of McDonald's obsession
Just not too much
And lots of resilience
And that's how it is!

Leiliana Rai (8)

Ruislip Gardens Primary School, Ruislip

This Is Me

I am a super swimmer
I am starting swimming season
I am a karate kicker
I am a singer
I am a karate boxer
I am a mysterious baker
And a cake baker
I am a game player
I am a sketch artist.

Maya Marcoci (8)
Ruislip Gardens Primary School, Ruislip

This Is Me!
A kennings poem

I am a...
Fast football player
Good basketballer
Good reader
Great swimmer
Healthy boy
Fit boy
Nice boy
Good helper
Love sweets
Love chocolate
Like games
This is me!

Alfie Lynas (8)
Ruislip Gardens Primary School, Ruislip

All About Me

I am...
A bookworm
A great gamer
A joker
A supersonic swimmer
A brilliant student
A sweet eater
A film watcher
A super sloth lover
Finally...
I am...
A fantastic friend.

Betsy Llewellyn (8)
Ruislip Gardens Primary School, Ruislip

This Is Me

There is something
You can watch it
It is called football
I love watching it
There is a game of it
There is even something
Called art
I am very good at it
I really like it.

Yamin Al Youssef (8)
Ruislip Gardens Primary School, Ruislip

This Is Me!

T alented footballer

H ugger

I am kind

S uper swimmer

I can be reliable

S inger

M e, perfect

E -sport-aholic.

George Rycraft (8)
Ruislip Gardens Primary School, Ruislip

This Is Me

A jump and a sprint
And I score a goal
My teammates
Are cheering me on
And another game comes
And we score again!

Mekhi Perry (9)
Ruislip Gardens Primary School, Ruislip

Number One Gamer

I am...
A football striker
A joker
A gamer
A YouTuber
I like Cobra Kai
I like to play PlayStation.

Harold Liko (8)
Ruislip Gardens Primary School, Ruislip

Gracefully Dancing

D ancing joyfully in my room
A crobatically twirling in the studio
N oting the main steps
C reating dance moves alone
I don't want to stop doing what I love
N o one can stop me from dancing
G racefully materialise on the liquorice-black stage.

Kyo Adachi-Mavromichalis (11)

The Japanese School In London, Acton

My Song

I see a ballerina dancing on the stage
I hear someone singing in a dark cage
I smell a red rose from under the singer's nose
I touch the key and open the cage
I taste sweet honey in my mouth
I feel my song all around me.

Hikari Inoue (11)
The Japanese School In London, Acton

Love Food!

H   ill is the goal of my picnic
U   sually, I have many sweets
N   ap on the hill
G   rowing vegetables is fun
R   estaurant is my favourite place
Y   oghurt is good for health and is delicious.

Yuika Kaji (10)
The Japanese School In London, Acton

Go For The Goal

I see a lonely goal on the field
I hear the turf's waves crash
I smell the rust of the goalposts
I touch morning dew on the turf
I taste the sweat on my lips
I feel sadness as it is so lonely.

Tomoharu Shigetomi (11)
The Japanese School In London, Acton

I'm Always Hungry

H amburgers are yummy
U sually, I study
N ow, I'm eating vegetables
G eography is fun
R eally too difficult homework appears to be
Y uto is my name.

Yuto Murata (10)

The Japanese School In London, Acton

Catboy

C atching fish is fun

A t the playground, I always run

T hrough tunnels is fun

B lue is the best colour

O ctober is my birthday

Y esterday, I played.

Shin Isoda (10)

The Japanese School In London, Acton

Flyfishing

I see the deep blue lake
I hear fish flopping for the fly
I smell cooked fish with butter and pepper
I touch colourless, sticky fish slime
I taste delicious fish
Flyfishing is such fun.

Ray Nestor Ito (11)
The Japanese School In London, Acton

I Like To Sleep

S ometimes I feel so tired
L ast night, I was so sleepy
E very day
E very night
P erfect blanket for me
Y awning, yawning!

Junichi Takahashi (9)
The Japanese School In London, Acton

Sleepy

S leepy, I said

L emons are sour

E lephants are big

E scape from the piano? Never!

P iano is my favourite

Y o-yo was fun.

Jinya Yatsu (10)
The Japanese School In London, Acton

Me

Q uite good at school
U sually, I swim at the pool
I like camels
E ating sushi is very fun
T ennis is my favourite sport.

Kaito Nakamura (10)

The Japanese School In London, Acton

YoungWriters® Est. 1991

YOUNG WRITERS INFORMATION

We hope you have enjoyed reading this book – and that you will continue to in the coming years.

If you're the parent or family member of an enthusiastic poet or story writer, do visit our website **www.youngwriters.co.uk/subscribe** and sign up to receive news, competitions, writing challenges and tips, activities and much, much more! There's lots to keep budding writers motivated!

If you would like to order further copies of this book, or any of our other titles, then please give us a call or order via your online account.

Young Writers
Remus House
Coltsfoot Drive
Peterborough
PE2 9BF
(01733) 890066
info@youngwriters.co.uk

Join in the conversation!
Tips, news, giveaways and much more!

f YoungWritersUK   **𝕏** YoungWritersCW   **⊙** youngwriterscw